Ricky Roogle

Super Coloring Book for Am@ng.us Fans

Bibliografische Information der Deutschen Nationalbibliothek:
Die Deutsche Nationalbibliothek verzeichnet diese Publikation in der Deutschen Nationalbibliografie; detaillierte bibliografische Daten sind im Internet über http://dnb.dnb.de abrufbar.

contact author: ricky.roogle@t-online.de

Herstellung und Verlag: BoD – Books on Demand, Norderstedt
ISBN: 9783752657715

SHHHHHHH!

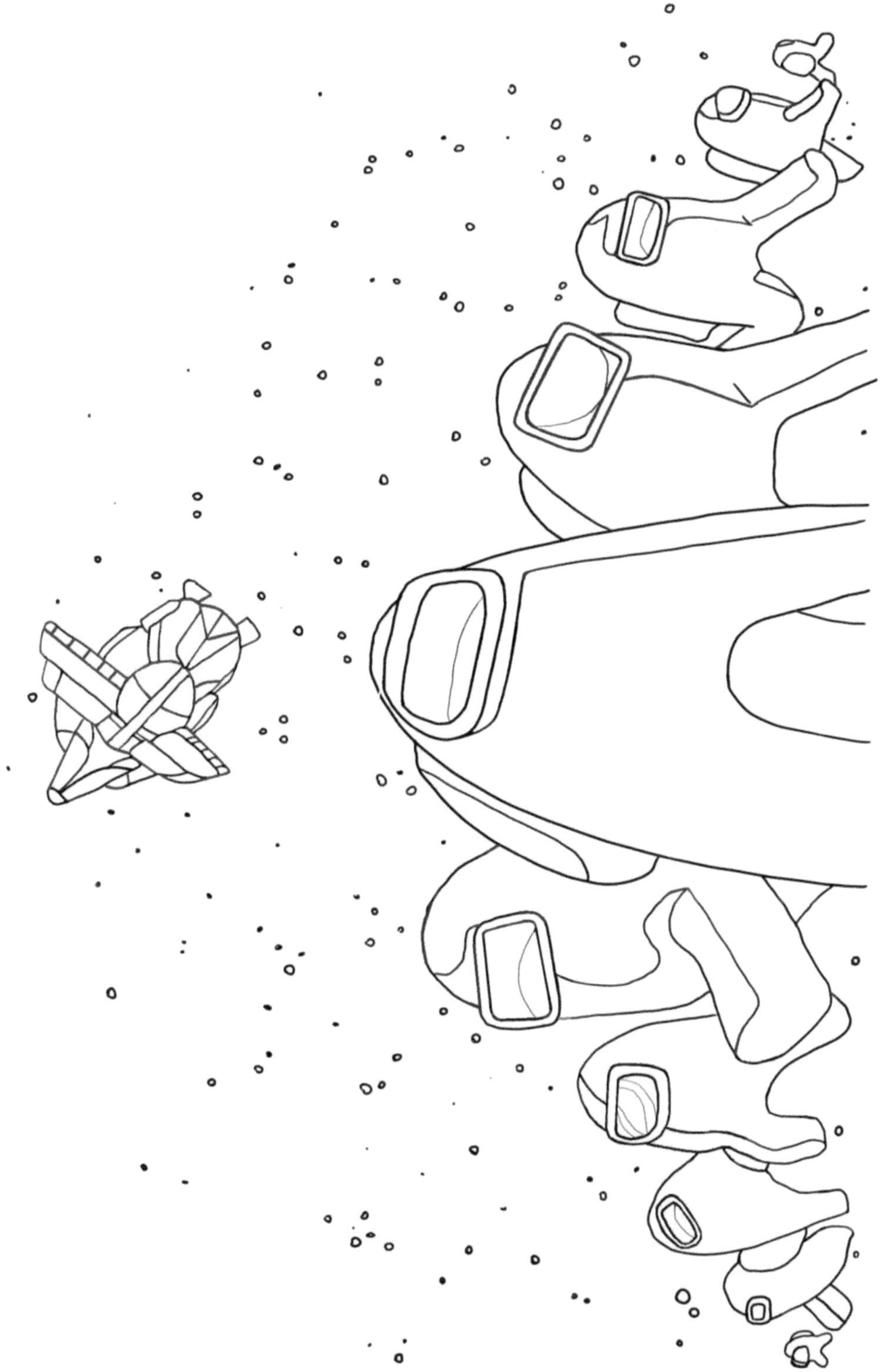

START
9/10

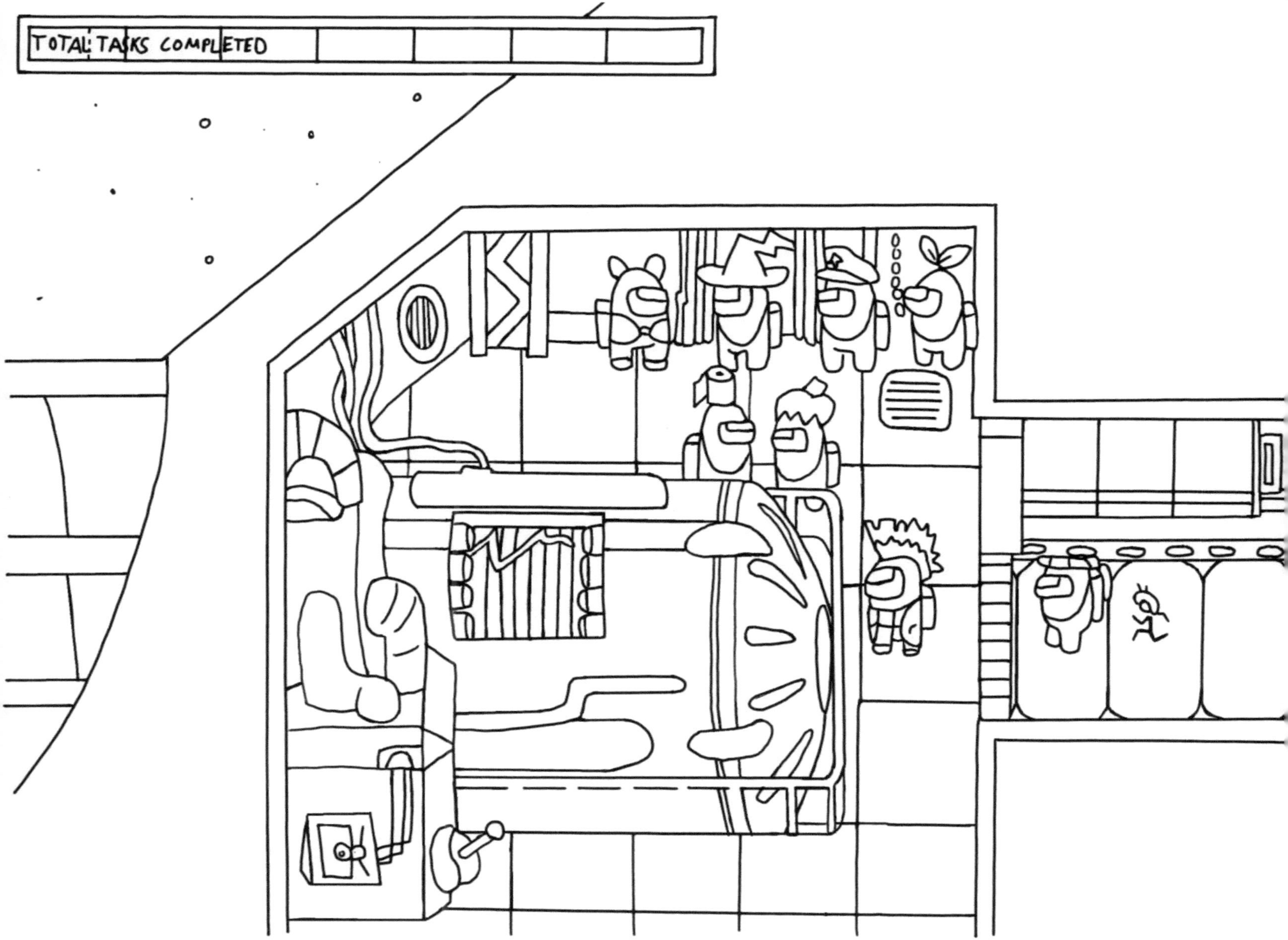
TOTAL: TASKS COMPLETED

Who I
tor?
DISCUSS!
SKIP VOTE
Voting Ends In: 72s

AMONG US

AMONG US
LOCAL
ONLINE
HOW TO PLAY
FREEPLAY

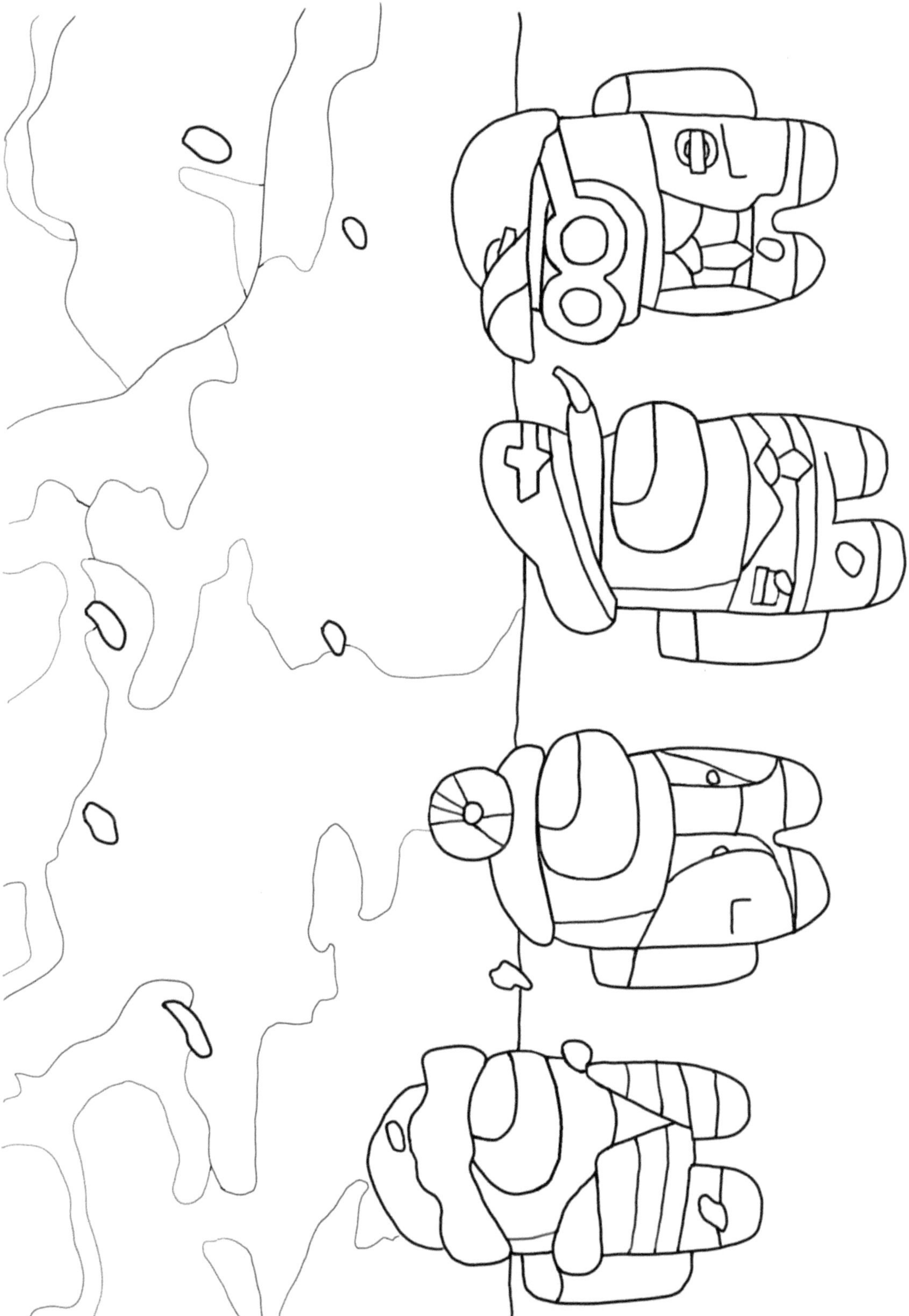

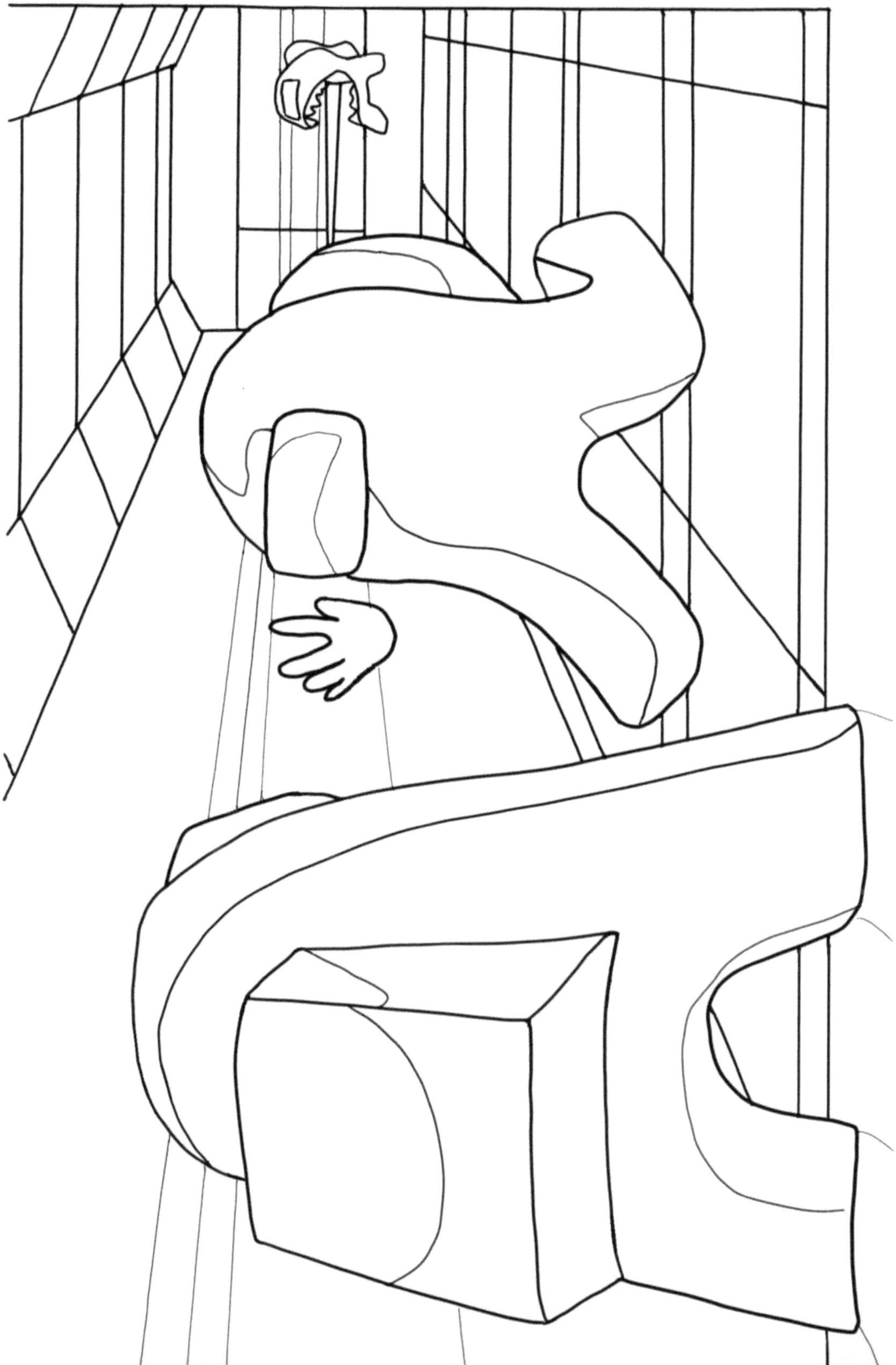

USE

TOTAL TASKS COMPLETED
TOO SLOW TRY AGAIN

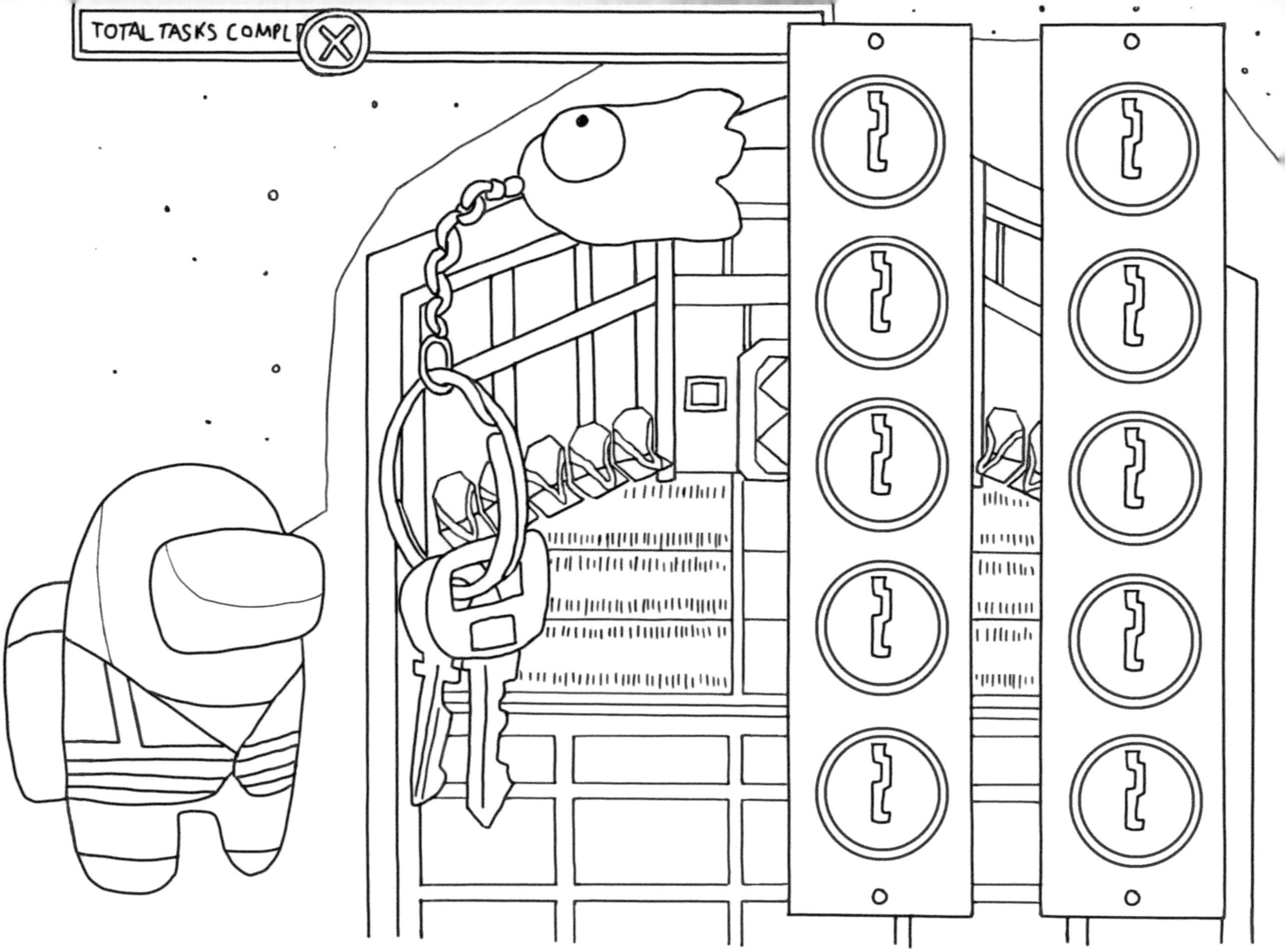
TOTAL TASKS COMPL

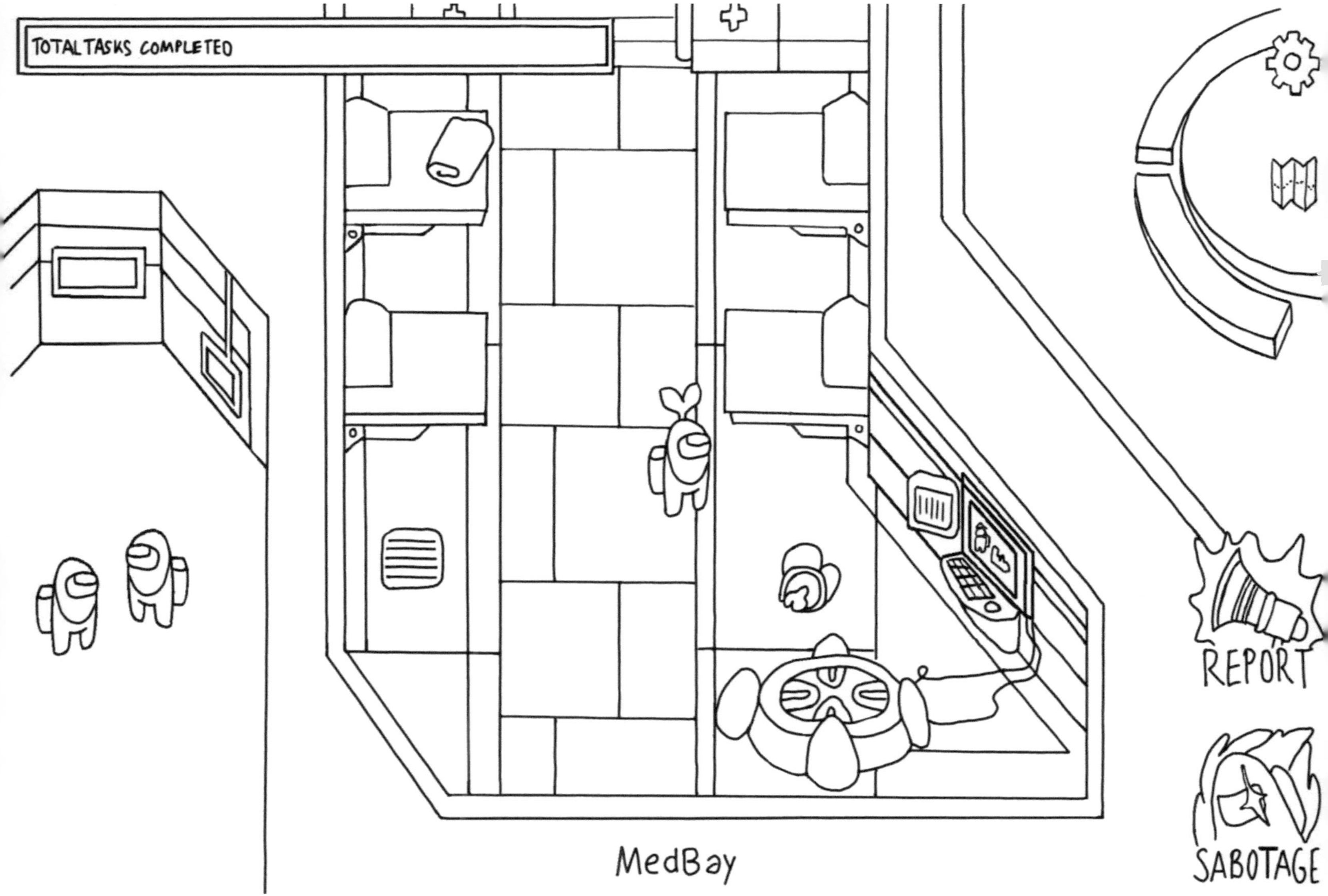
TOTAL TASKS COMPLETED
REPORT
SABOTAGE
MedBay

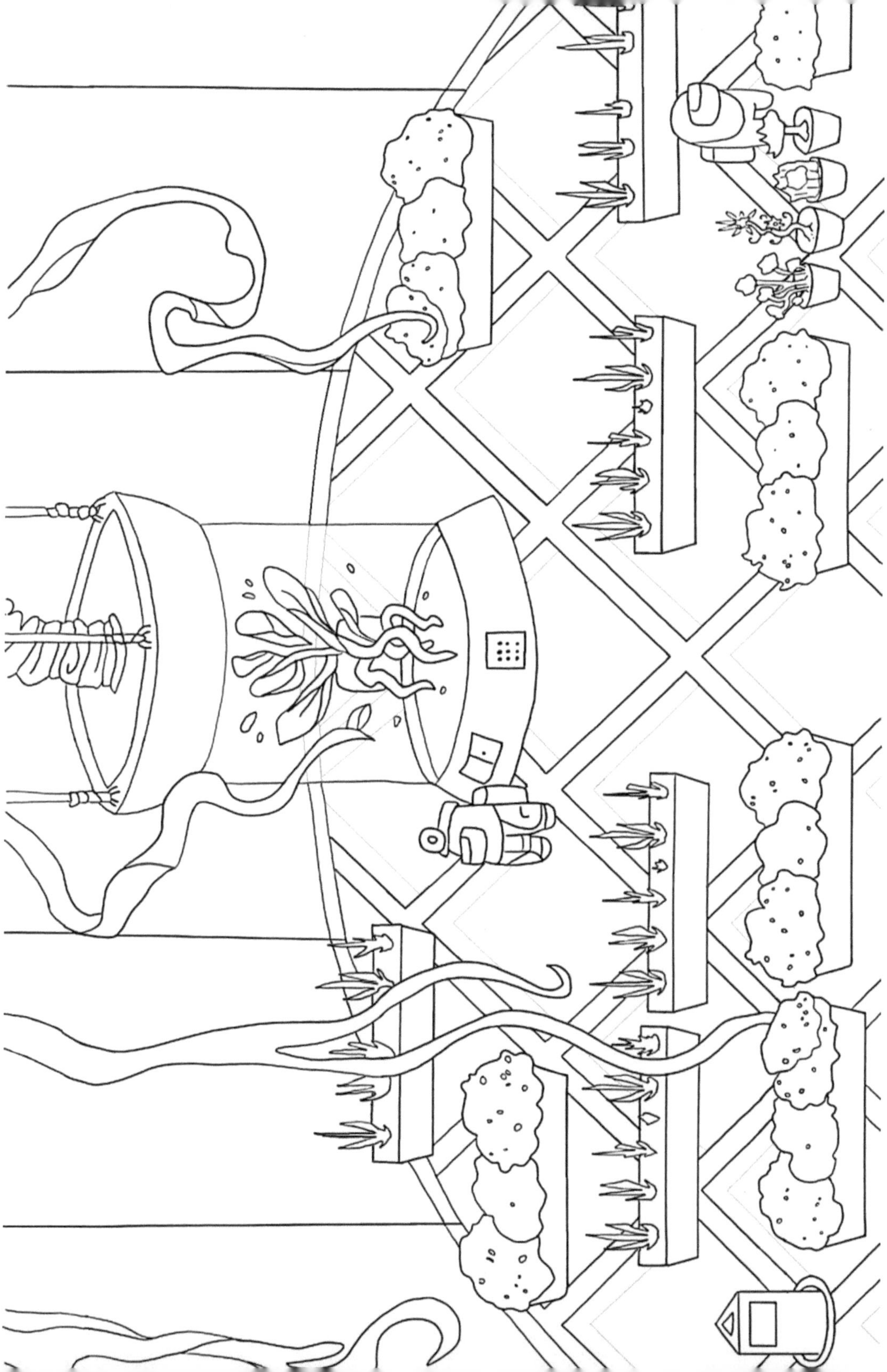

EMERGENCY
MEETING

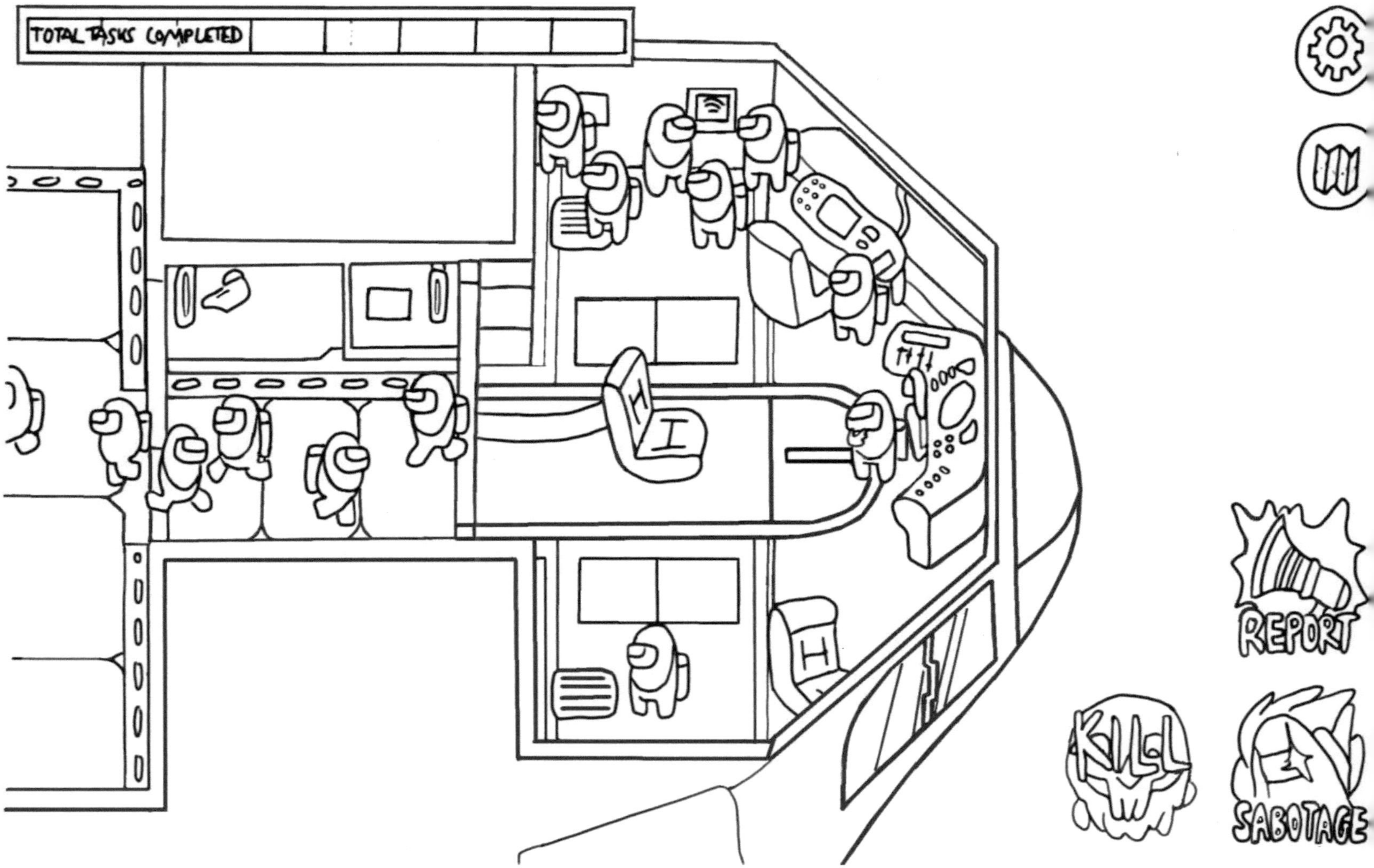
TOTAL TASKS COMPLETED
REPORT
KILL
SABOTAGE

SUPER
COLORING BOOK
for Ameng.us Fans

CREWMATES
COLORING BOOK
for Ameng.us Fans

The
SUPER
MAZE BOOK
for Ameng.us Fans

PASSWORD
LOGBOOK
for Ameng.us Fans

MATH
COLORING BOOK
for Ameng.us Fans

HOW TO DRAW
SKINS
for Ameng.us Fans

WORD SEARCH
PUZZLES
for Ameng.us Fans

SUPER
QUIZ
BOOK
for Ameng.us Fans
QUIZ

CARTOONS
MEMES and
JOKES
for Ameng.us Fans
WTF!

Notebook

Crewmate Notebook

Impostor
Notebook